£1.50

STEAM RAILWAYS
of Devon & Cornwall

Nick Luff

Bossiney Books • Launceston

This book is dedicated to my wife for her unswerving support and unbridled enthusiasm for trains!

Nick Luff

Acknowledgements

Many thanks are due to the following: South Devon Railway, Bodmin & Wenford Railway, Phoenix Railway Project, Bruce Hunt, Plym Valley Railway, Lappa Valley Railway, Launceston Steam Railway, Lynton & Barnstaple Railway, Imerys (Ivor Bowditch), Arthur Westington, Paul Burkhalter, Roy Wilce, Morwellham Quay Museum and staff, Bere Ferrers Railway (Chris Grove), Chris Wadey, Ray Bartlett, Geoff Husband, Cyril Thomas, Sam Downing, Eric Youlden, A & P Falmouth (Mike Reynolds), Pat Warner, David Weeks, Viv Wilson, Teignmouth Museum, Tiverton Museum, Museum of Dartmoor Life, GW Society (Bristol/Didcot), Delabole Quarry (Ian), Robey Trust, Trevithick Trust, National Railway Museum (York), Maurice Dart, Swindon Railway Museum (Tim Bryson).

First published 2004 by Bossiney Books Ltd
Langore, Launceston, Cornwall PL15 8LD

ISBN 1-899383-62-X

Introduction

I like trains. And yes, I'll admit it, I was a train spotter! Well, in the 1950s and 60s most boys were – how else might a 10-year-old encounter the likes of 'Luckie Mucklebackit' and 'Princess Arthur of Connaught'? As well as individual engines, the trains too had their own names: official ones, as in 'The Master Cutler' and 'The Irish Mail', and unofficial, such as 'Tavy Goods' and 'Perisher'. Branch lines were referred to by their local nicknames, the 'Tivvy Bumper' or the 'Slow and Dirty'. The railways were full of vitality and romance. It was not just the sensory spectacle of steam: they were an integral part of daily life and the landscape, more animated and comforting than the soulless 'people-movers' of today.

They also played a crucial role in the economy of Devon and Cornwall. Over the last 200 years the mineral wealth of the counties, mainly copper, tin and china clay, has been extracted on a vast scale. The only effective way of moving this bulk traffic used to be by rail and sea, and until the middle of the last century agricultural producers and, of course, the tourist industry depended upon an effective, integrated network of railways and tramways.

It is the richness and variety of this complex system and its dependency on a massive labour force that I've tried to capture in my pictures. And wherever possible I've related the historical with the contemporary. From the bucolic charm of a rural branch line to the magnificence of Brunel's architecture, from the impudence of a saddle tank to the majesty of a King class, the railways of Devon and Cornwall had a breadth and quality that were difficult to match. Slow and dirty they may have been, but they got the job done.

As we now head on into the twenty-first century, their character lingers on – the preservation movement is currently thriving, so much so that I feel quietly confident that steam railways do have a future. Steam trains will continue to assuage the pangs of nostalgia, and leaves on the line and the wrong sort of snow won't bring the wheels to a slithering halt.

It wasn't all picture postcards and painted stations whistling by —

Key to map opposite

Locations of pictures
(numbers are page references)

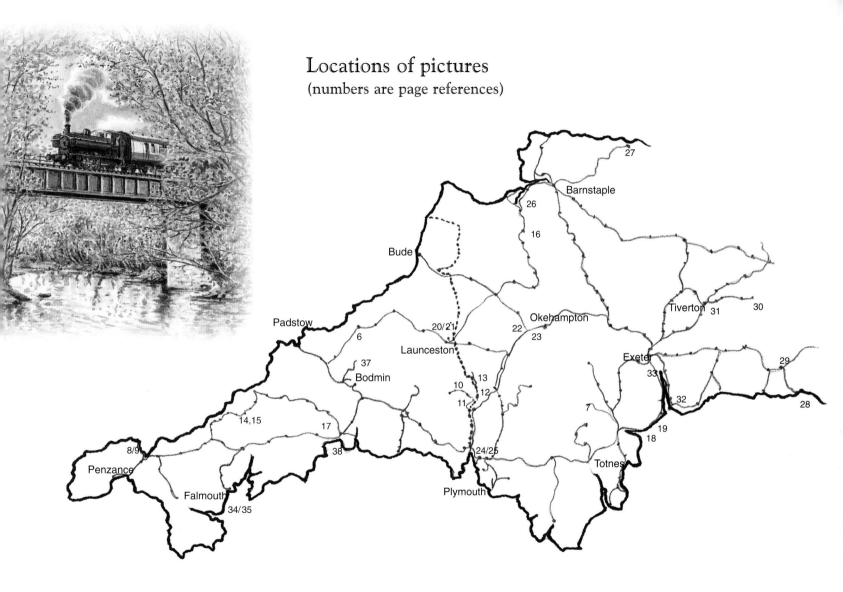

Rocks and hard places

Much of the building and construction work in the South West has been in local granite and slate, and the countryside is littered with the overgrown remains of quarries. Many workings were situated on the granite plateau of Dartmoor – around Haytor could be found a particularly fine-grained stone which was used extensively on many major edifices, notably London Bridge (now re-erected in America).

There were horse-drawn tramways and railways decades before steam locomotives. In 1820 the Haytor Tramway started transporting granite down 1300 feet to the Stover Canal 8 miles distant. The tramway was highly unusual (hence its inclusion here), with granite 'rails' instead of iron. Even pointwork was carved laboriously out of stone – centre foreground in the picture opposite shows a section of unused pointwork, with the moveable iron point-blade in place. The 'trains' ran by gravity where possible; a degree of braking was achieved by levering long poles against the wheels. Teams of heavy horses were also used both for braking and for haulage.

I've shown some loaded wagons being pulled out of the lyrically named Rubble Heap quarry on a bitter winter morning, with sunlit Haytor rocks on the horizon. The loading derrick is behind the 'train' and nearby a sweating horse is 'rugged-up'. The boulder (left foreground) displays the characteristic grooving caused by the feather and tare method of stone splitting, and two examples of implements used are lying on the rock surface.

◀ *Slate extraction has continued at Delabole, Cornwall, for centuries. At one time the quarry was claimed to be 'the biggest hole in Europe'!*

The view left shows 'John Allen', a Hunslet design of 1879, leaving the quarry head for the dressing sheds with a loaded train. It was one of a pair (the other was called 'E. Jago') and worked until the Great War.

The Cornish Riviera Limited

Since the late 19th century Cornwall has been a favourite destination for holidaymakers. The rail network had to expand to cater for this rapidly increasing traffic, and the most famous of the many expresses heading west was 'The Cornish Riviera'.

Always referred to by railwaymen as 'The Limited', this express used the most modern locomotives and luxurious rolling stock of its time. From 1927 it was usually hauled to Plymouth by a King class engine (see page 25) and onwards into Cornwall by a smaller 4-6-0.

On summer Saturdays the express ran through to St Ives. From St Erth it was double-headed by two 45XX Prairie tanks. The painting opposite shows it leaving Lelant station; the second engine is doing most of the work! A little further on, the branch line runs by the remains of Lelant quay, part of which is formed out of the hull of a First World War torpedo boat destroyer – possibly a veteran of the battle of Jutland in 1916.

The term 'Cornish Riviera' was coined by the Great Western Railway (GWR) publicity department in 1904 on the publication of a book designed to encourage people to holiday in Cornwall. A through train from London to Penzance, the 'Riviera Express', was introduced the same year but this soon changed to the 'Cornish Riviera Limited'. In 1957 the name was finalised as the 'Cornish Riviera Express' and so it remained until the title died with the introduction of regular interval expresses in the 1990s.

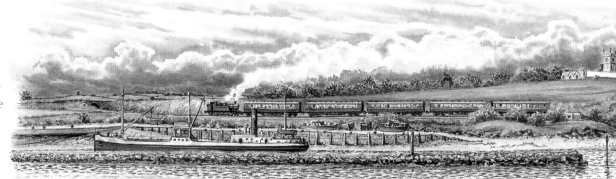

▶ *The branch train sauntering past a now crumbling piece of history on the far bank. The vessel in front is a small coaster used for shipping stone and china clay.*

The wreck of the 'Hesperus' and the little blue engine

▲ *Number 2 was converted to standard gauge in 1907 but only stayed for four more years as, in footplate parlance, 'it couldn't pull the skin off a rice puddin'. It was sold to the Selsey Tramway in 1912, rebuilt again and named 'Hesperus', but by now it was more a wreck than 'the most splendid star in the firmament'! It was scrapped in 1927. The Phoenix Railway at Seven Stones is today aiming to build a replica.*

The East Cornwall Mineral Railway (ECMR) officially opened in 1872 between Kelly Bray and Calstock for transporting minerals to the tidal river Tamar. Two 0-4-0 saddle tanks, built by Neilsons in 1871, operated the 3ft 6in gauge line. To avoid confusion, they were called Number 1 and Number 2 (shown left shunting the brickworks siding at Seven Stones).

By 1908 the line – now standard gauge – was reopened as the Plymouth, Devonport & South Western Junction Railway (PD&SWJR). Service trains were worked by three Hawthorn Leslie tank engines specially designed for the severe gradients and curves. Passenger trains were usually handled by an 0-6-0 with bright blue and red livery called 'A S Harris'.

An Edwardian PD&SWJR passenger train is shown opposite entering Chilsworthy station on its way to Kelly Bray (Callington). It has just shut off steam on the 1:40 climb into the platform. The unusual signal on the platform was operated by waiting passengers, or in this case a liveried chauffeur, to stop the train.

'Ada' on the Devon Great Consols Railway

This 5-mile line was built in 1859 to connect the large complex of copper mines on the Devon side of the Tamar valley to the quays at Morwellham. The Devon Great Consols Mine became the largest copper mine in Europe: this particular mining company was the only one to build and run a standard gauge line in Devon or Cornwall.

In 1880 two 0-4-0 saddle tanks called 'Ada' and 'Hugo' replaced the original Gilkes Wilson engines on the line. Built by John Spittles of Newport (who made only a few steam engines), they worked until the mine closed in 1901. 'Hugo' was scrapped shortly afterwards. 'Ada', however, was used when the narrow gauge ECMR was converted to standard gauge in 1907 by the London & South Western Railway (LSWR).

'Ada' was again used as a contractors' engine at Merrivale on Dartmoor in an unsuccessful attempt to connect the granite quarry with the GWR Princetown branch. This venture failed because of the effects of the Great War and the conflict was ultimately responsible for the final demise of 'Ada'. In 1915 it was sold to the Belgian Government for war work and was destroyed in the Flanders battlefields.

The painting opposite shows 'Ada' emerging from a short tunnel that was bored through a rock dump below Wheal Josiah Mine. It is about to plod its way up a 1:60 bank *en route* to the quays on the river Tamar. In the right foreground is a leat carrying water to one of the many water wheels in use at the mine. Crossing over this channel is a run of iron 'flat' rods that carried the energy generated by the water wheels to various machines, pumps and ore crushers on the site.

▲ *The George & Charlotte Mine Tramway at Morwellham Quay now takes visitors deep inside the old workings.*

The rush hour in 1950s Cornwall!

Situated almost one mile from the nearest village, this cruelly exposed halt (today still virtually intact but invisible amongst the greenery) was never well patronised at the best of times. Mitchell and Newlyn was the second of six very Spartan halts opened in 1905 by the GWR on the 1849 Cornish Mineral Railway line built by Joseph Treffry between Newquay and Chasewater.

Originally constructed in timber, they were later rebuilt in prefabricated concrete with a very bleak corrugated iron shelter perched on top. The painting opposite shows one of Colletts' versatile 57XX pannier tanks of 1929 vintage arriving with a Newquay 'stopper' (45XX Prairie tanks were more usual). On a blustery autumn evening a solitary customer eagerly waits to entrain. West Country passengers were always a hardy breed!

The westernmost part of the narrow gauge Lappa Valley Railway ends within 100 metres of Mitchell and Newlyn halt. Opened in 1974, this little line follows the old trackbed down the valley, passing by the ruins of East Wheal Rose engine house and its 120ft high chimney. Part of this lead and silver mine flooded in 1846 after a violent rainstorm. It was the worst mining disaster to occur in Cornwall, with the loss of 39 lives.

▲ *15" gauge 0-6-0 tank engine 'Zebedee' heading away from East Wheal Rose mine on its return trip up the river valley to Benny Halt.*

▲ *An elegant timber viaduct on the Torrington & Marland clay railway in Devon. The 3ft gauge line ran for 7 miles between ball clay workings at Peters Marland and the LSWR at Torrington. 'Mary', one of the 0-4-0 saddle tanks crosses the river Torridge. Sadly, the railway, its seven engines, the bridge and the heron are all long gone.*

Workers' playtime

In the painting opposite it's high summer in the early 1950s. The evening shadows are lengthening in Cornwall's Luxulyan Valley as the sultry stillness gives way to the staccato beats of steam engines working hard, the sounds reverberating from the lofty arches of a granite viaduct (in use until 1927).

In typically grimy condition, though only about 6 years old, a 'Modified Hall' class slogs up the 1:40 gradient with a summer holiday special from the West Midlands to Newquay. The engine is a Hawksworth development of Colletts' highly successful 'Hall' class of 1924. The large numerals on the smokebox are 'reporting numbers' to assist with train identification. With a full load of 280 tons, the train still requires the assistance of a banking engine at the rear.

The 57XX pannier tank 'banker' is passing beneath the 98 ft high Treffry Viaduct – built by the industrialist JT Treffry in 1843 (granite for its construction came from nearby Colcerrow quarry) to carry a horse-drawn tramway and canal over the valley; it was part of a complex of china clay lines that converged on Newquay and Par harbours. The entrepreneurial spirit of the GWR in the latter part of the 19th century turned Newquay from a small fishing village into one of the country's principal resorts. This growth in holiday rail traffic continued right up to the 1960s when the effects of mass car ownership led to a decline in the services.

The title of this piece, by the way, reflects my own experiences as a railway fireman in the 1960s. On a sunny day (not too hot though!) with a good mate and a nice engine, it was a delight to be at work.

Castles and stars

Brunel's broad gauge opened from Exeter to Teignmouth in 1846 and two years later his Atmospheric system was in use on this stretch. However, it proved expensive to operate and was scrapped after less than a year. In 1892 the line was converted to standard gauge using conventional steam engines. Herein lay the problem! Gradients were not too difficult for the Atmospheric train, so the whole line was constructed with ferocious banks of about 1:40, enough to make a normal locomotive have the vapours. Consequently, the heavier main line trains had to be assisted over the hilly bits by another engine, which was both time-consuming and costly. This practice continued regularly until the demise of steam in the 1960s.

Dawlish station in the late 1940s, shown opposite, was a favourite holiday destination. Passengers could leave the train and dangle a toe in the briny before the guard had blown his whistle. The express approaching is headed by one of Colletts' famous 'Castle' class 4-6-0s (a highly influential design of the steam age).

It is being passed by an 'up' van train being hauled (only just) by an ailing 'Star' class – a fore-runner of the 'Castles' by the same GWR engineer. Although a groundbreaking design, by the post-war period the Star's brilliance had been eclipsed by more modern engines. Having a bad trip with a rough engine, the fireman can be seen wrestling with a fire iron in an attempt to make things boil a bit better!

▶ *The 'Elephant', a 1924 Sentinel road tractor bought by the Teignmouth Quay Company to shunt wagons in the docks, which it did successfully from 1931 to 1963. I've shown it at 'Bobbets Corner', involved in quayside repairs. All the decoration and large lettering on the engine were made from crown bottle tops.*

The 'Ace' up the sleeve of the withered arm

The LSWR reached Launceston in 1886, a year after the Launceston & South Devon's broad gauge line. Each railway had its own station barely a lump of coal's throw apart. Wartime necessity led to a connection being made between the competing companies in 1943.

The link remained and until 1962 both railways used the South station. The whole of the Southern's 'withered arm' down to Padstow was lopped off by Dr Beeching in 1966. And, to add insult to injury, snow prevented scheduled trains from reaching Launceston – the last train to get there arrived after the line had officially been closed!

The Southern's principal train on this route was the 'Atlantic Coast Express' (always known as the 'ACE' by railwaymen), running from Waterloo to many destinations in the south west. The title, strictly speaking, is a misnomer, as one portion of the service ran through to Plymouth, which isn't exactly on the Atlantic Coast...

Invariably entrusted to a large Bulleid Pacific ('Merchant Navy' class) from London to Exeter, the smaller but very similar 'West Country' and 'Battle of Britain' classes usually took the Padstow section forward from Exeter. The scene opposite shows the down 'ACE' awaiting departure from Launceston South in the mid-1950s. The Train Staff or Token is being handed to the driver of the 'Battle of Britain' engine. This authorises the train to travel over the next single line section.

▲ *The Launceston Steam Railway now occupies 2 miles of the line. It uses 2 ft gauge Penrhyn quarry engines, one of which ('Lillian') is shown above, with the castle on the horizon.*

Er'l go if er'l start!

Steam engine sheds came in all shapes and sizes, but one thing they had in common was an aura of desolation relieved only by the animated appearance of the engines themselves. The engines might have been immaculate (sometimes) but their surroundings were definitely not. In 1949 at Meldon quarry, near Okehampton on the very edge of Dartmoor, the little shed was derelict and, appropriately, it was host to an equally moribund occupant, an Adams G6 class 0-6-0 tank.

Of 1894 vintage, these tanks were rugged shunting engines built for the LSWR. Unremarkable in every respect, they could be found in small numbers almost anywhere on the South Western. 30272 was transferred to departmental stock as DS3152 for use at Meldon where it staggered around until it threw in the towel in 1960 (the engine crews probably felt the same way when the G6 was replaced by another one, 30238). The railway came here in 1874 as part of the main line from Waterloo to Plymouth, but it was 1897 before railway engineers realised the quality of the rock they had driven the line through.

By 1959, at Plymouth Friary, another G6, 30162, could be found in an equal state of decrepitude (see page 24). It was usually attached to a wagon, because if the driver inadvertently stopped with the valves in a particular position it went neither backwards nor forwards. The shunter and fireman would detach the wagon, push it back a few yards, then ram the G6 to 'bump-start' it. Needless to say, it was not a popular machine…

▲ The short-lived 'Devon Belle' Pullman (behind an unrebuilt 'Battle of Britain' class Pacific), crossing Meldon Viaduct slowly in the early 1950s on its way from Waterloo to Plymouth.

Laira

The engine sheds at Laira were opened in 1908. This was where Plymouth's GWR fleet of passenger, goods and shunting locomotives were serviced and maintained. The depot was situated within a complex of Western and South Western lines on the east side of the city, and included a roundhouse and through-shed. It was a place of noise, smoke and general squalor, and was particularly unsavoury around the coal stage where (apart from replenishing the engines' coal stock) fires, smoke boxes and ash pans were cleaned.

But often something green and pleasant could be found there. Opposite is a view of the coal stage with an immaculate 'King' class being prepared for the up 'Cornish Riviera Limited'. 6015 spent most of its time based at Old Oak Common near Paddington, so it was a frequent visitor to Plymouth.

Behind 6015 is saddle tank number 1363. It was usually to be found clanking around the tortuous trackwork in Milbay docks until 1962 when it was placed at the end of a long row of engines at Laira waiting to be towed away for scrap. However, 'persons unknown' sabotaged it, so when its turn came to be towed away it stayed put – and there it stayed for a whole year. As it was the last survivor of the class, the Great Western Society stepped in and bought it.

Close to the engine shed were the goods yards and transfer sidings, a common sight in cities during steam days. Although engines could go all day on a tender or bunker full of coal, they had to replenish their water supplies several times during the same period. Consequently, water columns or towers were situated in stations and yards everywhere.

The toy train and the engines lost at sea

The Lynton & Barnstaple Railway (L&BR) was opened in 1898. At 20 miles, it was the longest passenger-carrying narrow gauge line in England. Despite the breathtaking scenery the 'toy train', as it was known locally, was rarely in profit.

Trains often took two hours to reach their destination and on one memorable occasion Lord Chichester, having missed the train, caught up with it on horseback 4 miles further on. The early morning train sometimes stopped to allow passengers to pick mushrooms! The line closed in 1935.

The four Manning Wardle 2-6-2 tank engines (and one American product) were named after local rivers, and there is a persistent rumour that 'Lew' exists on a coffee plantation in Brazil – but there's an awful lot of coffee in Brazil! The main illustration shows 'Exe' hauling a mixed train near Woody Bay station, which is now the centre of a preservation scheme resurrecting part of the railway.

Nearby, the short-lived Bideford, Westward Ho! & Appledore line opened in 1907. Its three Hunslet 2-4-2 tank engines were named 'Torridge', 'Grenville' and 'Kingsley'. Although of standard gauge, the 7-mile line was never connected to the main network at Bideford (LSWR) until, ironically, after the line closed in 1917 when the whole thing was requisitioned for the war effort.

◄ *One of the engines gingerly crossing over the River Torridge, on temporary track, on its way to the main line station, and thence to war. The other two wait their turn at the quayside terminus. It seems that 'Grenville' and 'Torridge' were lost at sea when their transport ship was torpedoed off Padstow.*

The 'Lyme Billy'

The 6-mile branch from Axminster to Lyme Regis was opened in 1903. However, because of its sharp curves and steep gradients, all the locos damaged either the track or themselves. In 1913 two LSWR Adams Radial 4-4-2 tank engines, dating from 1882, were tried with great success and they continued to work the difficult line (a third engine was added in 1946) until displaced by BR-built Ivatt 2-6-2 tanks. Dieselisation came in 1963, but in January and February 1965 two GWR 0-4-2 tanks were used to alleviate a shortfall in diesel railcars. One of the GW engines was 1442, the 'Tivvy Bumper' (see page 31). Complete closure occurred in November 1965.

With the Radial tanks, the same engine worked the branch trains for a whole week; Saturday was 'change-over day' when a fresh Adams tank took over. The main picture shows this happening with 30583, newly overhauled at Eastleigh works, leaving with the normal single-coach branch train while the other engine waits at the far end of the platform to return to Exmouth Junction shed.

On the main line an express from Waterloo to Exeter passes through, hauled by an unkempt rebuilt 'Battle of Britain' class. In the last few years of steam operation, engine cleaning (a job never sought after!) was rarely carried out – the cab sides were frequently the only part cleaned and this was usually done by the crews.

▶ *An Ivatt tank crossing Cannington viaduct. When still quite new, one span was reinforced with a jack arch due to fears of instability. Flagmen stood on the end of the viaduct to warn trains of landslips.*

The 'Tivvy Bumper'

There used to be hundreds of branch lines in the country and perhaps the quintessential example could be found at Tiverton in Devon, where two short branch lines diverged from the GWR main line. A 7-mile line following the River Culme to Hemyock was opened in 1876. Its meandering course resulted in a maximum speed limit of 15 mph and, with four intermediate stops, trains could take an hour to reach their destination. Following the introduction of electric lighting in trains, the carriages used on this branch were specially converted to gas because the speeds were too slow for the dynamos to keep the batteries charged.

The line closed to passengers in 1963 but remained open for milk traffic from the creamery at Hemyock until 1975 – an important revenue earner for the railway. The tank wagons, designed for use in passenger trains, were glass-lined so freight train work and loose shunting were prohibited. On this page a mixed train is going pell-mell along the river valley.

On short branch lines, to maximise efficiency, the Push and Pull or auto-train was often employed. This system enabled the engine to remain attached to the same end of the train irrespective of direction. In 1844 a 4-mile line was opened which connected what is now 'Tiverton Parkway' station with the town. It was originally called Tiverton Road ('road' being a railway euphemism for 'nowhere near'!) In GW and BR days the 'Tivvy Bumper' (opposite) used push-and-pull trains with a 'Donkey' 0-4-2 tank engine.

One of the line's stalwarts, 1442, is shown opposite, bowling along near Halberton. The fireman is probably half-cooked and half-frozen in the draughty engine whilst his mate luxuriates at the other end. When not constrained by speed limits, 'Donkey' tanks achieved 60 mph (probably downhill with a following wind, but then I'm a bitter old Southern man!)

The agony and the estuary!

Exeter was a very busy railway centre where the GWR and the LSWR main lines to the far west converged and separated again. Each company had its own principal station within the city, St Davids (GWR) and Central (LSWR). They were connected by a short but ferociously steep incline and it probably caused some glee to the Southern men that trains had to go downhill to reach the Western. A more serious consequence was that nearly all traffic had to be assisted by at least a pilot engine in front or a banker behind.

The daily perishable goods train from Plymouth to London was known as the 'Tavy Goods', perhaps because it carried much of the fruit and veg from the Tavy and Tamar valleys. The view opposite shows this important train arriving at Central station, helped in the rear by a 'Z' class 0-8-0 tank. Agonisingly slow, on the brink of the hill and just about to bust a gut with effort, is an SECR 'N' class 2-6-0. Dating from the 1920s, these strong engines were popular all over the Southern, though at speed (about 60 mph) it felt as though they had 'wheels like thrup'ny bits!'

Exeter was the origin of the LSWR Exmouth branch line, which opened in 1861. It was, and remains, a well patronised line. The picture on this page shows one of the South Western's versatile M7 0-4-4 tanks, of 1897 vintage, cantering along near Exton on its way to the resort in the 1950s. (Known to enginemen as 'Motor Tanks', M7s were fast and reliable.) On the other side of the Exe estuary the exhaust from a down Western Region train heads for Dawlish.

▲ *M7, 30676 – before being transferred to Exmouth Junction shed, it was based at Nine Elms in London where it was the 'Royal Shunter' for use at Waterloo when members of the royal family went by rail. Consequently, it was cleaned every day and, when not attached to the royal train, was restricted to shed duties to prevent its paintwork being spoilt. It was taken out of service in 1961.*

Tanks for the memory

Sorry about the pun, but saddle tank engines, oil tankers and oil tank wagons are all inextricably linked to the Falmouth Docks Railway in Cornwall. The internal railway system commenced operation in 1861 and two years later it was connected to the newly completed broad gauge Falmouth branch line.

In 1926 Hawthorn Leslie supplied four new 0-4-0 saddle tanks to replace three much older broad gauge engines. These old vertical boilered engines were re-gauged in 1892 when the GWR converted to standard gauge.

The illustration opposite shows Falmouth's 'Number 3' puffing gently off the Empire Jetty and pulling the dock's own fuel tank wagon, which was generally known as 'Dirty Dick'. In front of the engine are the paint-splashed keel-blocks used to support ships in dry dock, and behind is the Queen's Jetty, which burnt down in 2002.

'Number 3' was originally 'Number 1': they changed identities when they swapped their saddle tanks. By 1986 only 'Number 3' (ex No. 1) was left. It was the last commercially active steam engine in Cornwall and is now preserved on the Plym Valley Railway near Plymouth.

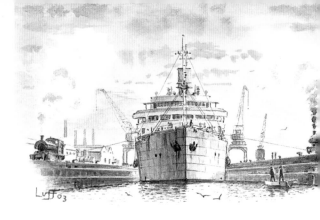

▲ *Apart from shunting duties, the Hawthorn Leslies were used in pairs to haul ships into dry dock, with a tug attached to the rear acting as a brake.*

Towing enormous loads like this was very heavy work for the little engines, and dangerous for the drivers and firemen. Large ships, usually tankers, could be caught by the wind and would start to drag the locos. A butcher's knife was kept in the cab to sever the hemp hawsers in case an early bath seemed imminent! Curiously, the knives remained on the engines long after this practice ceased.

I remember that our engines on the Southern Region carried large, completely useless spanners in the tool lockers – for hitting things which wouldn't work, and that might include the fireman!

'Ere mate, 'tis geddin' dimpsey up yer!

In 1863 W G Beattie produced a small 2-4-0 well tank engine for suburban passenger work on the LSWR. Although successful, all 85 were due for withdrawal from service by 1893. However three of them were reprieved and were despatched to the heart of Cornwall for use on the Bodmin & Wadebridge Railway (B&WR). Nearly 70 years later they were still working there hauling freight, mainly china clay. In more recent years two of the three engines were saved from final abandonment and, in 2002, 30587 returned to work on the now preserved Bodmin & Wenford Railway.

The Bodmin & Wadebridge Railway opened in 1834 and was the first in Cornwall to have locomotives. On the goods branch to Wenfordbridge trains had to stop *en route* to take water. The apparatus needed for this task was pure Heath Robinson – a spring-fed stream on the hillside above Pencarrow Woods was diverted through a cast iron channel to the lineside, and then via a leather 'bag' into the engine's well tank. Occasionally the activities of cattle at the spring head managed to divert the stream away from its normal course, so the train's water stop became a dry one! My illustration opposite shows 30587 taking water on the daily goods train to Wenfordbridge.

Drivers and their regular mates would sometimes swap roles to give the fireman some driving experience, but the fireman was often expected to make up the fire as well. Here the driver attends to the water bag whilst his fireman, having just attended to the fire, sits on the fence and has a cigarette. The driver remonstrates with his mate as he is about to disappear in smoke!

When a letter can mean so much

China clay extraction is a major industry in Devon and Cornwall. By 1900 a network of mineral tramways and dockside lines had been created and various types of engines were employed which could cater for the transport of this increasingly important product.

The construction of Par harbour began in 1829. Designed by the industrialist Joseph Treffry, its principal function was to convey tin and copper from the many mines in the area. As this traffic declined, that for china clay grew. Several early Treffry tramways converged on the harbour and there was a link to the nearby GWR.

'Punch' was a Manning Wardle 0-4-0 saddle tank that worked in the harbour area in the 1920s and 30s. The engine underwent several alterations during its working life and the illustration top left shows the rather ludicrous hinged chimney extension acquired at some time. It was finally put out of its misery in 1944.

The Bagnall saddle tank 'Judy' (bottom left) was supplied in 1937 to replace earlier engines. Originally it was to have been called 'Chough', but in a telegram to Bagnalls the first 'h' was omitted from the name. Bewildered as to why the purchaser wanted to call his brand new engine 'Cough', Bagnalls contacted Treffry who, somewhat confused, plumped for 'Judy' instead. Mind you, I do feel both versions have a certain aptness. 'Judy' and her identical brother 'Alfred' are currently on the Bodmin & Wenford Railway.

Preserved railways in Devon and Cornwall

If you would like to experience some of the West Country's rich railway heritage for yourself, a visit to any of the following will more than repay your time and effort. Ring beforehand to check opening hours and train timetables – many of the preserved railways close in winter, but they provide ample services during the rest of the year.

Bere Ferrers Railway, Bere Ferrers
telephone 01822 840044

Bicton Woodland Railway, Budleigh Salterton
telephone 01395 568465
www.bictongardens.co.uk

Bodmin & Wenford Railway, Bodmin
telephone 08451 259678
www.bodminandwenfordrailway.co.uk

Dartmoor Railway, Okehampton
telephone 01837 55667
www.dartmoorrailway.co.uk

Devon Railway Centre, Bickleigh
telephone 01884 855671

Lappa Valley Railway, Newlyn
telephone 01872 510317   www.lappavalley.co.uk

Launceston Steam Railway, Launceston
telephone 01566 775665

Lyme Regis Railway
www.lymebilly.org.uk

Lynton & Barnstaple Railway, Woody Bay
www.lynton-barnstaple-railway.org.uk

Morwellham Quay, Tavistock
telephone 01822 833808
www.morwellham-quay.co.uk

Paignton & Dartmouth Railway, Paignton
telephone 01803 553760
www.paignton-steamrailway.co.uk

Phoenix Light Railway Project, Seven Stones,
Callington   telephone 01579 382922

Plym Valley Railway, Plymouth
telephone 01752 330881   www.plymrail.co.uk

South Devon Railway, Buckfastleigh
telephone 01364 642338
www.southdevonrailway.org.uk

References

Mineral Railways of the West Country, T Fairclough & E Shepherd (Bradford Barton)

West Country Harbours (H J Trump)

Exeter to Newton Abbot, Peter Kay (Middleton Press)

British Railways Locomotives 1948, Chris Banks (Guild Publishing)

Devon Great Consols, R J Stewart (Tamar Mining Press)

The Tamar & Tavy Valleys, Terry Gough (Past & Present)

The Mines & Miners of Dartmoor, Tom Greeves (Halsgrove)

British Railways Past & Present No.17, David Mitchell (Past & Present)

Southern Steam (South & West), T Fairclough & A Wills (Bradford Barton)

Exeter to Tavistock, V Mitchell & K Smith (Middleton Press)

Devon & Cornwall in Old Photographs, Kevin Robertson (Alan Sutton Publishing)

Plymouth Steam, Ian Lane (Ian Allen)

The Withered Arm, T W E Roche (Forge Books)

Callington Railways, R Crombleholme *et al* (Forge Books)

150 Years a Railway Town, Iain Rice (Hawkshill Publishing)

The Building of the PDSWJR, Stephen Fryer (Fryer)

Archaeology of the Industrial Revolution, B Bracegirdle (Heinemann)

The GWR, 150 Glorious Years, P Whitehouse & D St John Thomas (David & Charles)

Railway Design (Vols 1 and 2), B Haresnape (Ian Allen)

Industrial Archaeology of the Tamar Valley, F Booker (David & Charles)

The Haytor Granite Tramway, Helen Harris (Peninsula Press)

Lost Ships of the West Country, M Langly & E Small (Stanford Maritime)

The Archaeology of Railways, P Ransom (World's Work)